Robots

Written by Rod Rees

Series Consultant: Linda Hoyt

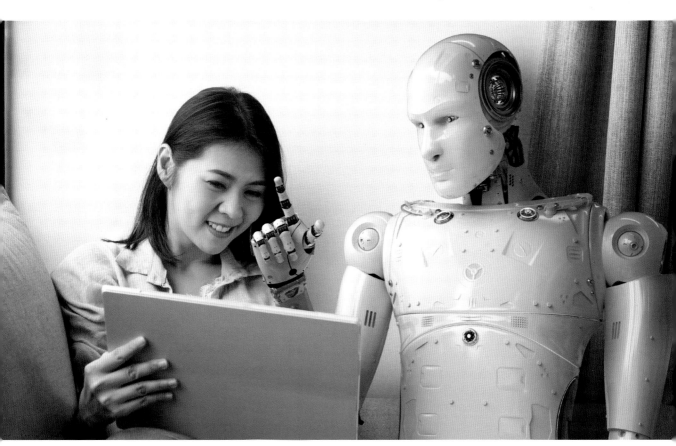

WorldWise
Content-based Learning

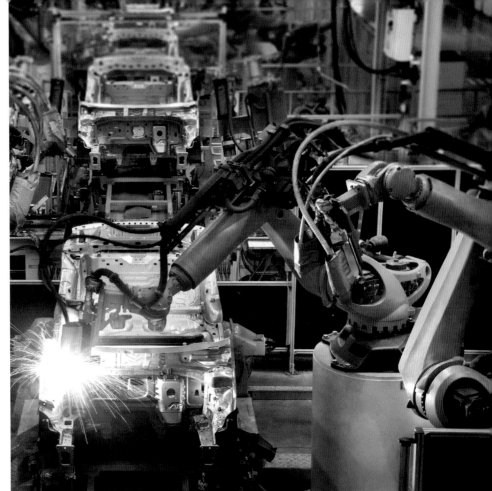

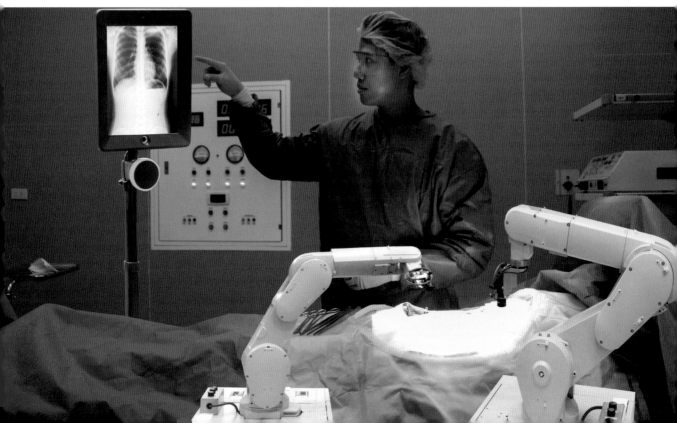

Contents

Introduction

Did you know that there are robots everywhere in our world today?

Robots are machines. They are programmed to work by themselves, and they have computers that tell them what to do.

Robots do work that is boring, difficult or dangerous. Robots help us in our daily lives.

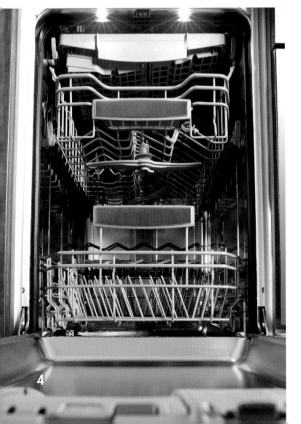

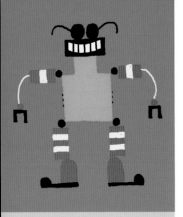

Chapter 1

Robots around the home

Some of the machines we use around the home are robots. If a machine is programmed to work by itself, it is a robot.

We use robots to do work we don't want to do, or don't have time to do ourselves. Robots save people time and energy because they can work by themselves.

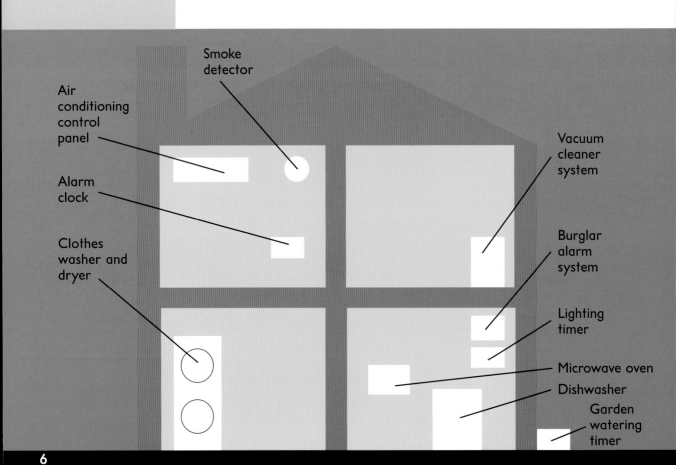

Smoke detector

Air conditioning control panel

Alarm clock

Clothes washer and dryer

Vacuum cleaner system

Burglar alarm system

Lighting timer

Microwave oven

Dishwasher

Garden watering timer

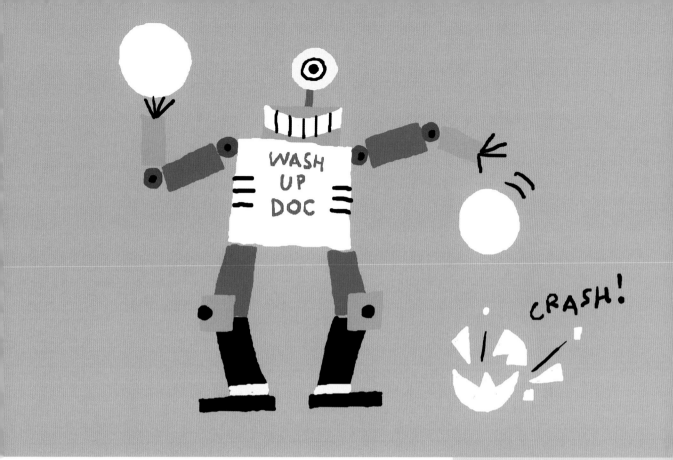

Robots inside the home

A dishwasher is a robot. It can wash and dry the dishes by itself. A dishwasher knows what to do because it has been programmed to carry out all the steps needed to wash dishes.

When a dishwasher is turned on, it starts to wash the dishes. When one part of the job is finished, it does the next part of the job. It keeps doing this until the cycle has finished and all the dishes are washed and dried.

Think about it

Do you think there will ever be a robot that loads and unloads the dishwasher?

A robot has been programmed to clean the floors in your home all by itself. It is smart enough to move around tables, chairs and other furniture.

Swimming pools need to be cleaned often. Cleaning a pool takes a person a long time, the work can be difficult and boring. But using a pool-cleaning robot that can do the job by itself makes it much easier to keep a pool clean.

A pool-cleaning robot can do what a person cannot do — it can stay under the water all the time. When the robot is turned on, it can clean all the hard-to-reach places in the pool.

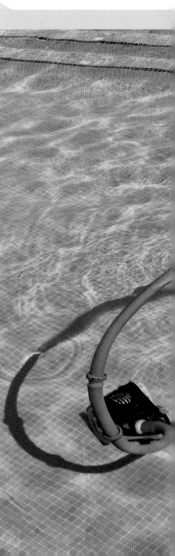

Another type of robot that you can have in your home today can actually talk to you and do many things. It looks like a speaker. This very helpful robot has a microphone that listens to your voice and can follow your instructions. You can ask it to tell you about the weather, play your favourite songs, or turn on your favourite TV program or some other device in your home. It can even remind you about something you need to do.

Developers are constantly coming up with new things that robots can do in the home. What do you think they will come up with next?

Find out more
What other robots are used around the home?

These robots clean airport floors.

Autonomous Cleaning Equipment
Capable of floor scrubbing, these equipment can clean floor faster and cover a wider surface area.

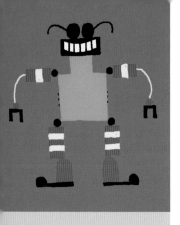

Chapter 2

Robots in the workplace

Robots are used in many **workplaces**. They can be programmed to make all kinds of things and to do many different tasks.

Robots are used in **factories** to put things together. They can be used to make cars and trucks. Robots can help perform operations and daily tasks in hospitals.

Robots in factories

There are many different robots for all the tasks that are done to make cars.

One robot puts on the car doors, another robot puts in the windscreen and a different robot puts in the steering wheel. Other robots put together the parts for the car engine, and robots also spray paint the cars.

People still need to work in factories to make sure that nothing goes wrong, but robots can work 24 hours a day, seven days a week.

Think about it
Do you think robots will ever drive cars?

Robots in hospitals

Robots are used in hospitals. They can be very important in medical operations. During an operation, the doctor uses a computer with **remote control** to tell the robot what to do. A tiny **robotic arm** can get to hard-to-reach parts of a human body much more easily than a person can.

Doctors sit near the patient and control the robotic arms that do the work. A camera allows the doctor to see inside the patient's body.

When a robot is used to do a medical operation, the patient gets well more quickly, suffers less pain and has a smaller scar.

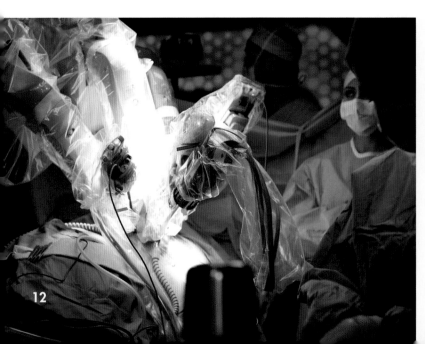

Find out more

What other things are robots able to do in hospitals?

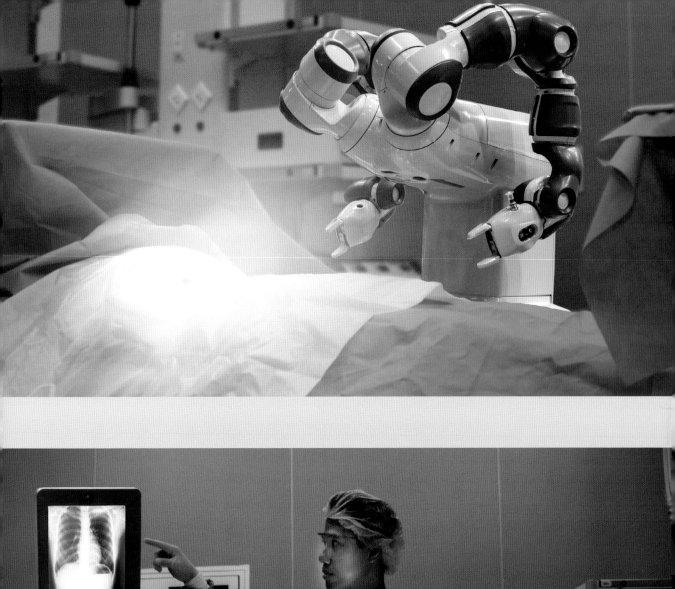

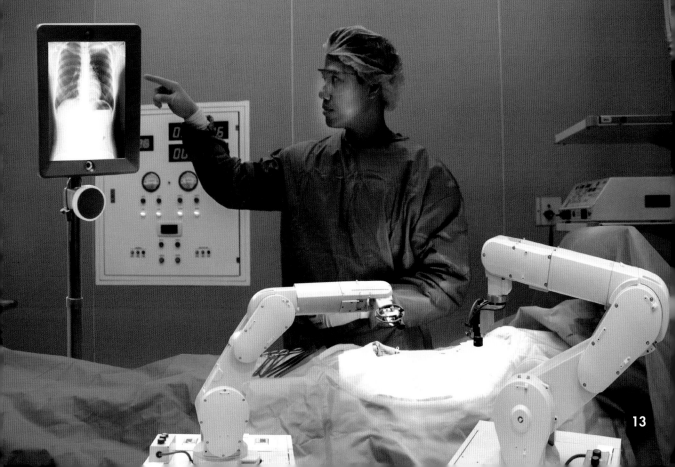

Chapter 3

Robots in dangerous places

People can use robots in places that are too difficult or too dangerous for humans to get to. Robots can be used to explore places and gather information, and also help in rescues.

Robots can be explorers

Scientists can send robots to explore places and gather information they need.

Robots can go deep underwater to explore the bottom of the ocean. This can be a much safer way for scientists to learn more about the ocean environment.

Robots can move around coral reefs to find and inject poison into starfish that have been killing coral.

Exploring a volcano is a risky
business, but sometimes robots can
be used to help. They can be used
to collect rocks or take photographs.

Robots can even be sent into space
to gather and send information back
to Earth for scientists to study.

Robots can help in rescues

Robots can enter burning buildings to locate where fires are and send out live video. Firefighters then use the information they see to quickly make a plan to put out the fire. They also use the video to help them search for people who are trapped inside.

Robotic drones can find the location of a **bushfire**. They send live video to firefighters showing how dangerous the fire is to people and property near it.

Robots can assist with locating people on mountains covered by **avalanches**. Rescuers use robots to make their job safer and to find people more quickly.

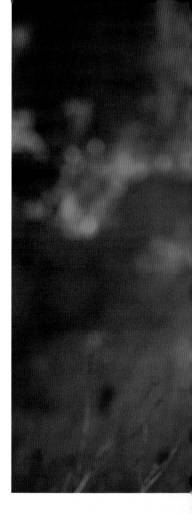

Conclusion

Robots are used around the world every day. But they can only do things they are programmed to do. Robots can follow instructions and work by themselves, but they can't think for themselves.

Robots are useful for doing difficult or dangerous jobs. They can also do boring jobs that need to be done over and over again.

Robots are very useful machines.

Glossary

avalanches huge amounts of snow, ice and rocks falling down a mountain, burying everything in their path

bushfire a large fire that is out of control

factories places where things are made

robotic arm a robot that can be programmed to move in the same way as a human arm

remote control a device that controls something from a distance

volcano an opening in the earth's surface through which ash, melted rock and poisonous gases pour out

workplaces places where work is done by people or robots

Index